BEYOND RULES

God As You Never Imagined

BEYOND
RULES

God
As You
Never
Imagined

DAVID GREGORY

One Press
Katy, Texas

Beyond Rules: God As You Never Imagined

Illustrations by Beckett Smith
Cover design by Jun Ares
Interior layout by Sandra Jurca

Published by One Press, Katy, Texas
www.davidgregorybooks.com

ISBN-13: 978-0-96751-416-1

9 8 7 6 5 4 3 2 1

Printed in the United States of America

HOW THIS BOOK
CAME TO BE

Books come from the strangest places. This one origi-
nated in a dinner conversation a few months ago at a
tiny place barely on the map in southeast Wyoming
called Woods Landing. It's not even a town, actually.
It's a country resort, with a river, and hills, and distant
mountains, and cabins, and a restaurant, and a post
office that I'm not quite sure is operating anymore.
Oh, and all around, hundreds of square miles of beau-
tiful Wyoming open spaces.

One evening, four of the young people there (two
of mine, and two of our hosts') devoted their dinner
conversation to God's purpose for our lives, and align-
ing ourselves with that purpose. (These are not your
average young people.) I sat nearby listening for five
minutes, and then, plate in hand, I adjourned to the
porch, not wanting to impose upon their conversation.

I was so impressed with their chosen topic, however, that I decided to follow up with one of my sons, the youngest of the group, and share with him what I had come to understand about it. So I sat down to write a letter. Soon I had the makings of a short book, one that several friends encouraged me to publish immediately, because they had young people in their lives that they wanted to give it to.

What you're holding is that book.

Although originally written to a teen, I decided not to put "teen" in the title or subtitle. We never grow too old for what is really the most important topic in life. May God use this short book to speak both to teens and former teens.

I, certainly, have been deeply touched simply by the process of putting these things on paper. Although, with all deference to the wisdom of God's timing in our lives, on a purely human level I do wish this: that someone had shared these things with me when I was 16.

David Gregory
MARCH 2023

a letter to my son

A few weeks ago I did an Amazon search on advice books for teens. Your birthday was coming up and you were turning 16 and, as a teenager, you're having to make decisions that will affect the course of your life. So I ordered a book, but after it arrived I looked through it and thought, "Meh."

Don't get me wrong. I'm sure it had plenty of good advice. But it seemed it could pretty much be summed up like this: Make sure you're well prepared to make a living. Choose friends wisely and be a good friend. Maintain a good relationship with your parents. Don't get hooked on destructive behaviors. Be a person of character and competence.

OK, I admit, those are pretty good suggestions. I'll probably give you the book, anyway. We can all use good input. But I got to thinking, if I'm trying to help you prepare for the rest of your life, why stop at that level? Why not go deeper?

You may be thinking: *Those five things seem fairly deep to me. I mean, aren't career prep, relationships, personal growth, character, and competence pretty important?*

They are. But they aren't the deepest things.

The deepest things have to do with what you, Truett, Nathan and Sarah started talking about a few weeks ago in Wyoming one night at dinner. Dig deep enough, and that conversation really had to do with issues like this—issues I think almost every teen (and almost every adult) has about life:

> *I wish I liked myself more*
> *I wish I felt really loved*
> *Sometimes I feel bad about things I've done*
> *Sometimes I feel . . . stained*
> *I wish I felt close to God*
> *How can I live the right way?*
> *Do I really want to do what's right?*
> *I just wish I had THE answer to life*

The amazing (or daunting!) thing about being human is that we can't escape these questions. They're built into our DNA, so to speak. At some level, every person on earth tries to answer them.

But how? The world doesn't offer us any ultimate answers. It doesn't even pretend to. So it provides self-help tips: be kind to yourself; don't beat yourself up about your mistakes; be the sort of person people want to be with; be true to yourself.

Again, probably good advice, but not exactly *the* answer to life. A lot of people take this route, though. To them, it seems like the best one available.

Conventional religion offers different answers: Keep these rules. Practice these rituals. Perfect these disciplines. Read this book. Say these prayers. Do all this stuff, and you, too, can connect with the Ultimate, the Divine. Plus, you'll get rewarded with heaven. Or paradise. Or nirvana. It may not seem like it where we live, but a lot of the world takes this route.

But honestly, is what you see of religion around the world (or around our neighborhood block) all that appealing? Does it really seem to answer these deep questions for people? Or is it, to some, simply the more appealing of the two alternatives, though it doesn't work very well?

So let's ask the obvious question: are there any other options?

I'd like to pose a thought experiment. Let's assume God exists. He's all-powerful, and he's perfectly loving. Under those circumstances, which is more likely to be true?

> ➤ God knows our need to have these deep
>   questions answered, but he's done nothing to
>   answer them. Basically, we're on our own.

> ‣ God knows our need to have these deep questions answered, he's provided the answer, and he's made that answer clear for us.

I'm writing to say that the second answer is not only the more logical of the two; it's also the truth. God really has provided the answer to the issues that your conversation in Wyoming raised. That answer has been right in front of us all along. Unfortunately, it's been buried for so long under so much religious stuff that figuring it out seems impossible—unless we go back to what God promised in the first place. Then it all becomes clear.

God's answer to our deep life questions is almost certainly not what you expect it to be. But once it's laid out, I think you'll see how it makes perfect sense, and answers our deepest longings in a way that's truly amazing. I think you'll see that God's answer fulfills the ultimate objective of virtually every religion and philosophy in the world. In other words, it's *the* answer.

I'm writing to simply lay it out clearly for you.

What you do with what I say here is totally up to you. You may legally still be a minor, but I'm not in charge of what you do with God. You are. I just want to make sure that you fully understand what you're deciding about.

My real hope is that you'll not only understand how God has answered these questions, but *experience* the answer to them. Hopefully, at a much younger age than I did it. If you do, your life will never be the same.

I'm not going to try to make this come across as something a teen would "relate to" by using the phrases people your age use or pretending I know exactly what life is like these days for teenagers. All of that would just come across sounding kind of dumb. I'm just going to try to be honest and straightforward.

I guess the bottom line is that we both want our lives to be meaningful and fulfilling, and I've come to realize that life really can be that way. So what I've come to know and experience, I'm simply passing on to you, that you can have a better opportunity to experience it, too.

What God offers us is far better than *try hard to keep God's rules, strive to be like Jesus (even though you'll never measure up), do plenty of religious stuff, and thank God that one day you'll get to go to heaven.*

That approach to life is *not* what God promised. What he offers is way better than that. You don't hear much of what God actually promised, though, because honestly it's just too radical. It's too far out there. People are more comfortable with a watered-down message.

In every generation, though, there have always been some who have said, "I'm going to believe what God actually says. I appreciate what others have taught me, and how they've poured into my life, but I know that God has more."

This letter is about that "more." Is it radical? Yes. Is it for you? Yes. Does it involve doing a lot more religious stuff for God? No. But it does involve understanding a whole lot more about what God has done for you.

I've found that what God actually says doesn't fit the small, preconceived boxes that we've constructed for him. To hear God's truth, I had to trash the boxes. I'm hoping you will trash yours, too.

A LITTLE HISTORY ABOUT RULE-KEEPING (TO SET THE STAGE FOR THE ANSWER)

When people think of religion, they usually think of rules. The Ten Commandments. The Five Pillars of Islam. The Eightfold Path of Buddhism. *Here are the things you have to do—or not do.*

But God doesn't operate by rules. I know, that's completely counterintuitive, but it's true. He operates based on promises. His promises.

God created humans to be receivers of his infinite love and to have the closest possible connection to him. But humans essentially told God, "We think we can find something better." They broke their connection with him. We see the result of that all around us. The world is a mess.

God became someone we run from rather than run to, because he was perfect, and we were so imperfect, and we thought it was best to simply keep our distance.

It's like how we joke that our guinea pigs seem to live in a constant state of terror. They like it that we feed them, but despite our best efforts to treat them tenderly, they're never quite sure that we won't eat them.

God never intended that we keep our distance from him. It's the opposite of what he created us for. So God committed everything he is, and everything he has, to this one purpose: reconnecting us to himself. We couldn't do it ourselves. Only he could. And he did it through a promise.

God started by making himself known 4000 years ago to a man named Abraham, who lived in Ur, an ancient city in southern Iraq. God made Abraham a promise: "I will make you into a great nation ... and in you all the families of the earth will be blessed." God termed this "an everlasting covenant." It was an arrangement that wouldn't go away. It was a promise that God *would* fulfill.

(BTW, in the back, I've included the Bible verses I refer to in this letter.)

Abraham believed God, and the Bible says that because of that, "God credited it to him as righteousness." Which means, "You have right standing with me, Abraham; everything is fine between us. You and I are OK."

Abraham hadn't done anything to earn any of this. He didn't keep a bunch of rules. God simply made him a promise.

But didn't God eventually give people rules? you may ask. He did. Four hundred years later, God gave Abraham's descendants, the Jews, 613 commandments to keep. Not just ten. 613. The arrangement was this: if they kept all of his commandments, he would bless them. If they didn't, he wouldn't. They all responded, "We will keep every one of them!"

Right.

They failed miserably.

So why did God give all those rules? To show people they couldn't reconnect with God by keeping rules!

God knew that, deep down, people realized they were missing something. He knew that every person had all of these deep, unanswered questions. And he knew that people would try to find what they were missing through rule-keeping. That's what people do. So he gave them all those commandments to show them that was *not* the way. No one could keep all the rules. No one could meet God's perfect standard. No one could reconnect with God by trying to be good enough. *That way would never work.*

The rules were a *temporary* arrangement. God gave them to make people ready for the real solution— a solution only he could provide.

Fast forward another 700 years or so. God's people hadn't kept his commandments, and things weren't going well for them. That's when God told them what to expect next. He said to them, "One day I'm going to provide you a new way—an entirely new arrangement between me and humanity." The temporary arrangement would come to an end. God's permanent answer would be revealed. His plan to reconnect us to him would be accomplished. It wouldn't be based on rule-keeping. It would solely be based on a promise. God's promise.

The new arrangement would be nothing—nothing—like the old one. And it would provide the answer to every one of our deepest questions.

AN ALMOST PERFECT ILLUSTRATION

I've been trying to think of a good illustration of God's answer to all of our most important questions. God's answer isn't complicated (it's actually very simple), but I've realized that an illustration would be a huge help. And I came upon one.

God's answer to our deepest questions is like a Saturn V rocket. That's right—the one used in the Apollo program to get astronauts to the moon, the one in the movie *Apollo 13*. The Saturn V is the largest rocket ever built: 363 feet tall, 33 feet in diameter, almost 3000 tons. We stood next to one at NASA on the south side of Houston, remember? It was beyond huge. Even lying on its side, it towered over us, as tall as a three-story building.

The Saturn V had three main stages, each with its own engines. Each stage was critical for the mission.

THE SATURN V

The first stage burned for two and a half minutes, lifting the rocket off the launchpad and 38 miles above earth. Its task completed, it detached and fell back to earth. The second stage burned for six minutes, accelerating to 15,500 miles per hour and lifting the rocket to an altitude of 109 miles. Its task completed, it detached and fell back to earth. The third stage burned twice: two minutes to get the ship into earth orbit, and then, later, five and a half minutes to achieve a velocity of 25,000 miles per hour and propel the spacecraft to the moon. Its task completed, it detached, leaving only the command module, which housed the astronauts, and the lunar module that would take two of them to the moon's surface.

For the purpose of our illustration, we'll pretend that the Saturn V had four stages (counting the two Stage 3 burns as one stage each). I don't think NASA will mind too much.

A NEW ARRANGEMENT

So God promised a completely new arrangement between him and humanity. Back then, the internet wasn't quite yet available, so God revealed how this new arrangement would work through two Hebrew prophets, Jeremiah and Ezekiel. God himself would bring it into being. It would be both for God's original people (the Jews) and everyone else (the Gentiles).

And it would be something that no one before ever imagined.

The very first thing God said about the new arrangement was absolutely essential. He said that the new arrangement would *not* be like the old arrangement, the one he had with people under the Law of Moses.

> "Behold, days are coming," declares the Lord,
> "when I will make a new covenant with the
> house of Israel and the house of Judah, *not*
> like the covenant which I made with their
> fathers on the day I took them by the hand to
> bring them out of the land of Egypt . . ."
> – JEREMIAH 31:31-32, EMPHASIS ADDED

Putting the old arrangement (the Law of Moses) and the new arrangement next to each other would be like putting the Wright brothers' first-flight airplane next to the Saturn V. The goal is to get to the moon. Standing next to these two craft, we'd say, "Well, the Wright brothers' plane has a lot to do with flight. It was a necessary step in the process. But it's not getting us to the moon. *It's not designed for that.*"

The Law of Moses had a lot to do with God. It reflected his character. And it was a necessary step—showing us how we fall short of God's standard. But it wasn't designed to get us where God wanted us to go in this life (or eternally, either). For that, we needed something completely different.

What does this mean for us? It means that to whatever degree we operate as if we're under the old type of arrangement—if I keep the rules, God will bless me; if I don't, he won't—we're in the wrong flying machine! It's *not* going to get us where we need to go. We are *not* under that kind of relationship with God. God did away with that for us. If we think that's how God acts toward us, we're not understanding God, and we're not understanding God's new arrangement.

So if God's new arrangement isn't like the old, what is it, and how does it resolve all of the really deep issues of life? God tells us. I'll go through these one by one, in slightly different order than the questions I listed earlier. I think you'll be amazed at how God has already answered every one of these issues for us. I was.

"SOMETIMES I FEEL BAD ABOUT THINGS I'VE DONE"

To get astronauts to the moon, the Saturn V rocket had to get off the ground. That's what Stage 1 did. It had the biggest engines on the rocket—five of them. They provided 7.7 million pounds of thrust, enough to lift 3000 tons 38 miles off the earth. That's a lot of power.

Stage 1 of God's new arrangement is powerful, too. Under the new arrangement, God said,

> "I will forgive their wrongdoing, and their sin I will no longer remember." – JEREMIAH 31:34

Wow. God won't even remember our sins anymore. That's a lot of forgiveness.

STAGE 1: FORGIVENESS

God knew we would need that much forgiveness. All of us have broken God's moral law. The penalty for that is death—separation from God. The penalty had to be paid. But God didn't want us to pay it; he loved us far too much for that. So he chose to pay the penalty himself. That's what Jesus did on the cross. God the Son, God in human form, paid the penalty for us.

So what do we have to do? Simply receive the gift. That's all we can do. God's forgiveness is only offered as a gift. There's nothing we can ever do to earn it. We receive this gift by faith—trusting that Jesus Christ is who he says he is, that he fully paid the penalty for our sins, and that he rose from the dead on our behalf. As John 3:16 says:

> "For God so loved the world, that He gave His only Son, so that everyone who believes in Him will not perish, but have eternal life."

If we've placed our faith in Jesus, all of our sins—past, present, and future—are already forgiven. Jesus put away the sin issue between us and God. It's completely removed. That's what "their sin I will no longer remember" means. As the Apostle Paul says, God no longer takes our sins into account. As his children, God treats us according to His love, not according to our sins.

Do you see how freeing this is? As a teen, you've done plenty of things you knew were wrong. We all have. We feel bad about things we've done. We wonder, *can God really forgive me?* We wonder, *how can I stop feeling bad about what I've done?*

Jesus's death on the cross is the answer. There, God provided 100% forgiveness. We don't have to live in guilt anymore. We don't have to keep condemning ourselves. God has wiped the slate clean.

But what about that really bad sin? we think. God doesn't remember it. Paul himself was a murderer. He killed Christians. But he met Jesus, and after that he knew that God no longer took his sins into account. He said, "I forget what lies behind, and reach forward to what lies ahead."

When Stage 1 of the Saturn V finished its job, it detached and fell back to earth. Its job was done. It didn't ever have to be repeated. When Jesus died on the cross, our sins were forgiven. That job was done. "It is finished," Jesus said. It doesn't ever have to be repeated. We are completely forgiven! We don't ever have to do anything to "activate" our forgiveness. Jesus already activated it.

The sin issue between you and God is done. You don't ever have to be focused on how you've fallen short. You don't ever have to wallow in self-condemnation. Because of Jesus, God doesn't condemn you for anything. Why should you?

Jesus came to deliver us from focusing on sin at all. He has something much better for us to focus on.

STAGE 1 IS FINISHED

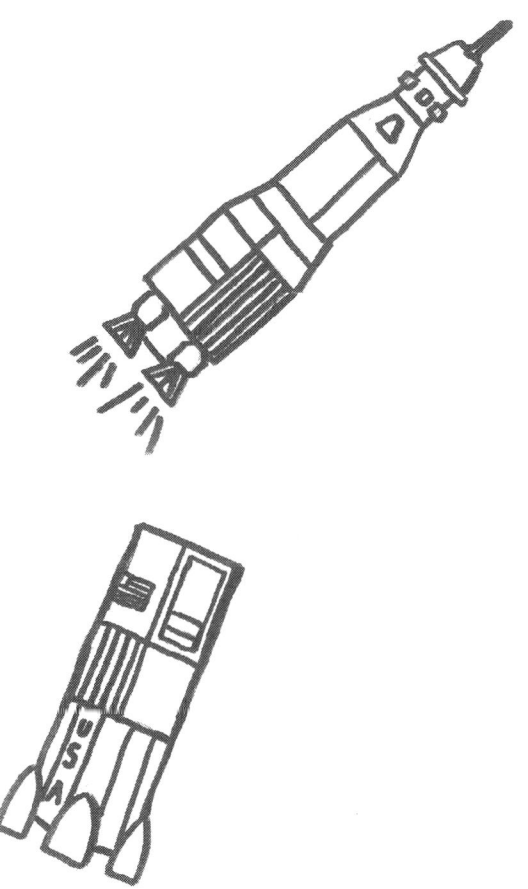

Unfortunately, forgiveness is often where the message of God's new arrangement with humanity stops. But stopping with forgiveness is like having the Saturn V lift off the launchpad a few hundred feet and then Mission Control in Houston announces, "That's good enough! Let's call it a wrap!" Until someone standing in the back asks, "Uh, weren't we planning on going to the moon?"

Forgiveness is just Stage 1. There's a whole lot more to come.

"SOMETIMES I FEEL ... STAINED"

Stage 2 of the Saturn V got it going much faster and much higher—over 15,000 mph and 109 miles up. Now this thing was really moving.

Here's stage 2 of God's new arrangement:

> "I will sprinkle clean water on you, and you
> will be clean." – EZEKIEL 36:25

It's fantastic to know that our sins have been fully forgiven, forever. That's a big deal. But even if our sins have been forgiven, it's still possible for us to feel stained on the inside.

God knew this. Sin pollutes us. It's like cars from the 60s and 70s. Some of them looked great, but man, did they spew out the pollution. You could tell by how black their tailpipes got. Fortunately, cars have gotten a lot cleaner since then. But not nearly as clean as God makes us.

God cleanses us completely when we place our faith in Christ. He washes us thoroughly on the inside. He doesn't give us half a bath. He makes us sparkling clean.

STAGE 2: CLEANSING

Once again, do you see how incredibly freeing this is? We are completely clean. Always. There's never a time when we aren't clean enough for God. There's never a time when we aren't good enough to approach him. There's never a time when, because we think we've performed badly, we have to "clean ourselves up" for God. Jesus already did that for us! He makes us completely worthy. That's why our Father says to us, "Approach me boldly. Be confident! I've made you clean. I *want* you to come to me—anytime, anyplace."

God washed us for that very purpose, so we could be close to him. He wants to be close to us, no matter how we think we've performed. It's not about our performance—ever. It's about Jesus's performance. It's about the free gift he gives us: the gift of being utterly clean on the inside.

Once Stage 2 of the Saturn V completed its task, it detached and fell back to earth. Stage 2 didn't ever need to be repeated; it was done. Once we are cleansed by God, that is taken care of. We don't need to do anything anymore to be clean. We *are* clean. We don't ever have to feel stained again. In my experience, when God makes this real to us, that feeling of being stained goes away. It's a lie, and it's been replaced by the truth. We are clean, now and forever. We can be at peace in that.

So we've been totally forgiven and we've been totally cleansed. We're ready for Stage 3.

"I WISH I LIKED MYSELF MORE"

For the Saturn V, Stage 3 was the final preparation stage before the spacecraft headed for the moon. The Stage 3 engine of the Saturn V burned for two minutes and propelled the spacecraft into earth orbit.

Getting into orbit is a huge deal. It means you can turn the engines off and get everything ready to go to the moon. The spacecraft will orbit the earth on its own, its forward momentum perfectly balanced by the pull of gravity from the earth, so that it simply keeps "falling" around the earth. It's pretty amazing, actually.

Stage 3 of God's new arrangement is a huge deal, too, and is even more amazing.

Many teens—the large majority, probably—really struggle with feeling that they aren't good enough. I know I did. In response, our culture tries to tell teens: Don't put yourself down! Think well of yourself! And that message is fine, in its place.

But the truth is this: if we're separated from God, in the deepest part of our being we're really not OK. That's true whether we're a teen, a 30-something, or an 80-something. The sad truth is that we're all born into the world with hearts in rebellion against God. We're sinful. We're self-seeking. We set ourselves up as our own god.

God loves us, yes, but our hearts are not OK. You can tell that by just glancing at today's news headlines on your phone. Humanity is a mess. Something is dreadfully wrong on the inside, and no amount of societal change and no number of new laws can fix it.

For us to be everything God intended us to be, God had to fix our heart problem. Otherwise, eternity would be populated by a bunch of forgiven people who were still rebels at heart, enemies of God. That's not exactly what God had in mind.

What does God do to fix our heart? Does he try to reform it? Improve it? Rehabilitate it? Not at all. He does something much more radical. He removes it entirely, and gives us a completely new one. In other words, he performs a heart transplant. Under the new arrangement, God promised this:

> "Moreover, I will give you a new heart and put a new spirit within you; and I will remove the heart of stone from your flesh and give you a heart of flesh." – Ezekiel 36:26

What is a heart of stone? It's hard. It's dead. It's unresponsive. That's exactly how God says we were born into the world—dead to him, unresponsive. What is a heart of flesh? It's alive. It's beating. It's warm. It's responsive.

God promises to take out our heart of stone and give us a heart of flesh—a heart that is alive and responsive to him.

God isn't talking metaphorically here. He's not talking symbolically. He's talking *literally*. He's talking about *reality*. When we place our faith in Christ, God does a genuine miracle inside us. He removes that dead inner being from us, and gives us a new, living inner being, one that is on his side, in complete sync with him.

STAGE 3: A HEART TRANSPLANT

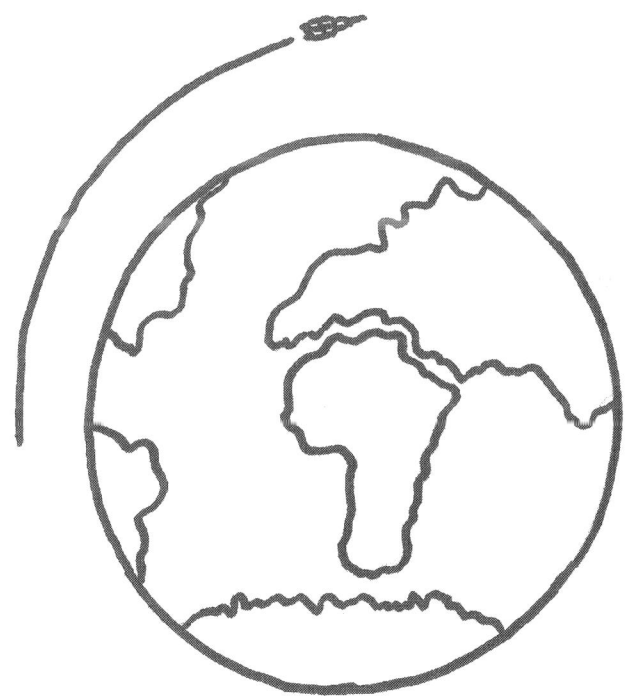

I remember clearly how I experienced this when I came to faith in Christ. All of a sudden, things were genuinely different. I had a peace and a joy I'd never had before. I cared about people in a way I never really had before. For the first time, overnight, the Bible made sense to me. And I really could recognize the leading of the Holy Spirit.

Something drastic had happened inside me. If someone comes to Christ at an earlier age, that's often not apparent. But I think my experience is typical of people who come to Christ as adults. They know something has changed. Because it has.

So how, exactly, does God perform this heart transplant? You can go online and see how a heart surgeon performs a physical heart transplant. How does God perform a spiritual one?

Jesus explained to a man named Nicodemus that the Holy Spirit actually births a new human spirit within us. He said that to be part of God's kingdom, we have to be born again, or born from above.

Jesus isn't talking about turning over a new leaf, or experiencing something in life that "feels like I've been born again." I so fell in love with a girl the summer after my senior year that I probably could have said, "I feel like I've been born again!" But I hadn't been. I was still the same, just filled with a lot of "in love" hormones that summer.

No, Jesus is talking about an actual birth in the

spiritual realm. The Holy Spirit gives birth to a new human spirit inside us. That's why over and over the New Testament writers speak of us as being "born of God." We are—literally! God gave birth to our new spirit (our heart of flesh). At the same time, he removed our old spirit (our heart of stone).

The Apostle Paul refers to these as the "old man" and the "new man." Our old man, he says, is gone. It no longer exists. We are the new man now. That's why Paul says about us:

> Therefore if anyone is in Christ, he is a new creation; the old things have passed away; behold, new things have come. Now, all things are from God ...   – 2 CORINTHIANS 5:17-18

The person we were before, with a sinful heart opposed to God, has ceased to exist. We are literally a brand new person.

God *had* to do a heart transplant on us to accomplish his plan. We couldn't be genuinely connected to God with our old, nasty heart. Which is why God did away with it.

The new heart God birthed within us is the opposite of the old one. It has God's own nature. "Flesh gives birth to flesh," Jesus said to Nicodemus. That is, humans give birth to humans. What we give birth to is like us. "Spirit gives birth to spirit," Jesus continued. That is, the Holy Spirit gives birth to our new spirit. Which means our new spirit is *like him*. It has God's nature. The Apostle Peter says we are "sharers in the very nature of God." Paul says that our new man is "created after the likeness of God in true righteousness and holiness."

(As I write, I sit here, amazed. I share God's nature! You do, too!)

Teens always struggle with their self-image. *Am I good enough? Am I cool enough? Will anyone really like me as I am?* (Here's a secret: adults struggle with self-image, too.)

The new birth is God's *complete* solution to the issue of self-image. God says to you (and me), "You're totally OK. I gave birth to you, and I don't give birth to anything that isn't perfect." Our behavior isn't yet perfect, but our new heart is exactly the way God wants it to be. You're not just accepted by God (although you are). You are now totally *acceptable* to God. In the depths of your being, you're completely OK. There isn't anything you need to do to make yourself more acceptable to him. He's already done it all for you.

Ultimately, what God says about us is the only thing that matters. And—I can say this from experience—what he says actually can become how we think about ourselves. That means we can be at complete peace with who we are. We can like ourselves, just as we are. We don't have to try to make ourselves into someone good. We *are* someone good. Very good. God birthed us that way. Which is fantastic news.

We're almost ready to journey to the moon. We have one stage to go.

"DO I REALLY WANT TO DO WHAT'S RIGHT?"

At this point, the spacecraft is orbiting the earth. However, the Saturn V wasn't designed just to get astronauts into earth orbit. It was designed to get them to the moon. For that to happen, it needed Stage 4 (which, actually, was simply the second burn of the rocket's Stage 3).

For Stage 4, NASA calculated the spacecraft's proper flight path from its earth orbit, determined the exact timing, and fired the engine, accelerating the craft to 25,000 miles per hour, propelling it to the moon. It was the last major step before the real objective could be accomplished: landing the lunar module on the moon.

Stage 4 of God's new arrangement was the last thing he needed to do before his major objective could be accomplished. When he gave birth to our new heart, God did something very special with it. What God promised in Stage 4 of his new arrangement was this:

> "I will put My law within them and on their heart I will write it." – JEREMIAH 31:33

The moment of our new birth, God actually wrote his law on our heart. That's kind of an incredible statement, but what law is he talking about here? Is he talking about the Law of Moses? God gave Moses 613 laws. Are each of those laws written on our heart? Is something written on our heart that says, "You shall not eat shrimp"? Or "Don't boil a young goat in his mother's milk"? Not exactly. Remember, God said that his new arrangement with us would *not* be like the Law of Moses. He's hardly going to promise that, then turn around and write the Law of Moses on our heart!

What does it even mean for something to be written on our heart? It means that's the passion of our heart. That's what we truly want to do. That's our deep desire. If we say of someone, "His patriotism is written all over his heart," that means patriotism is *really* important to him. If we say, "Her love for her husband is written all over her heart," that means she *really* loves him.

So what is written on our heart? Shortly before he was crucified, Jesus said to his disciples, "I'm leaving you with a new commandment: love one another, as I have loved you." The Apostle John wrote that Jesus only left us with two commandments: to believe in him and to love one another. That's it. Paul and James wrote that God's whole law is summed up in one command: love one another. James called it the law of liberty. Why? Because loving others is not, in the end, burdensome. It's incredibly freeing. It frees us from selfishness, and hatred, and bitterness, and indifference. It frees us to live with real peace and real joy.

God has written these two things on the depths of our heart: to trust him, and to love others. We *want* to do those things. Our new inner being *loves* to do those things. They bring us joy. In the depths of our being, *we are on the same page as God.* We're not in conflict with what he wants. We used to be, but we aren't that way anymore.

STAGE 4: GOD'S DESIRES IN OUR HEARTS

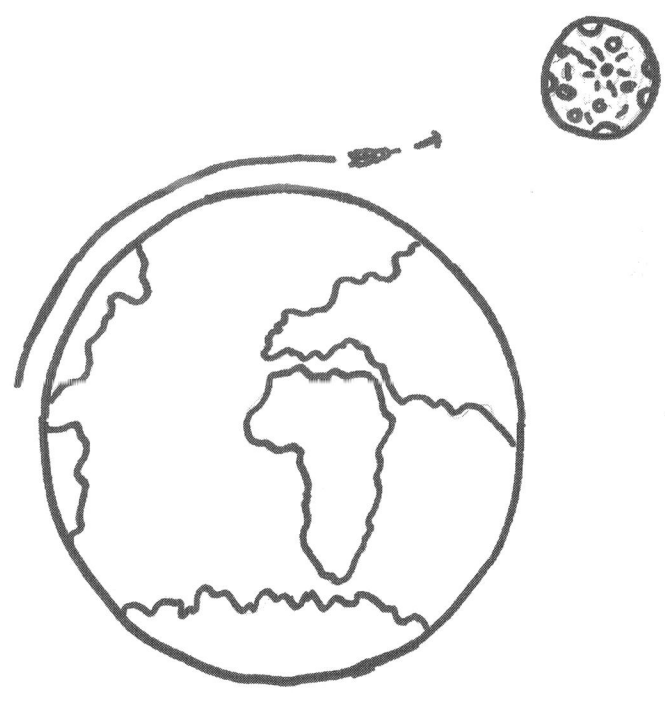

Having a new heart, and God's desires written on it, doesn't mean that we can never have thoughts or feelings that conflict with what God wants. What it means is that those things are *not* coming from our deepest being—the new creation we are in Christ. We *don't* truly want the wrong things. It may seem like we do, but as the Holy Spirit shows us what we truly want in a situation, we'll see that it matches what God wants.

Why is that important? Because it means that we aren't fighting a civil war against ourselves! When we say *no* to something wrong, we aren't saying *no* to our deepest desires. We're saying *yes* to them. Which is incredibly freeing! The Christian life is not one of constantly saying *no* to what we want. It's constantly saying *yes* to what we truly want in the depths of our being— because God wrote those desires there.

(You're probably thinking, *OK, if I have a new heart that's on God's side, with his desires written on it, why do I still sin?* That's a very good question, and God gives a very specific answer, which I will get to in a bit.)

Never again do we have to question, "Do I even want to do what's right?" or "Do I really want what God wants?" The answer to that question is always *yes*. If it doesn't seem like it, we haven't dug down deep enough, to our true desires.

In our new heart, we want what God wants. It may take a while to learn to get in touch with those deepest desires instead of our surface-level thoughts and feelings—that's part of growing up in Christ. But we can be at peace, knowing that we want to do the right thing. God has written it on our heart.

SO WHERE DOES THAT LEAVE US? AN UPDATE ON OUR SATURN V ROCKET

We've gone through all four stages of our Saturn V rocket. Stage 1 got us off the ground (complete forgiveness). Stage 2 got us going really fast (complete cleansing). Stage 3 got us into earth orbit (a complete heart transplant). Stage 4 propelled us toward the moon (God giving us his own desires).

Of course, for the Saturn V rocket, each of these stages took time. For us, God does them all instantaneously when we receive Christ by faith.

So if God has gone through all four stages, he's attained his objective, right?

No, not at all. All of those were incredible miracles God did in us. But they were simply the necessary steps to get us where God wanted to take us. They were not ends; they were means.

The point of the Saturn V rocket was not to get a bunch of metal into space. It was to get astronauts to the moon. The point of our forgiveness, cleansing, heart transplant, and new desires is not simply to have those things—though they are fantastic! The point is for God to achieve what he does next. Because what he does next is what he's been aiming for all along.

"I JUST WISH I HAD *THE* ANSWER TO LIFE"

Now the astronauts get to the moon—their true objective. Everything accomplished on the mission so far has been for the purpose of achieving this.

It's the same with God's new arrangement. Everything Jesus accomplished on the cross and through his resurrection, he did so that God could achieve this next promise. When we fully understand it, we'll see that it is God's answer to *all* the questions we listed earlier—and more. It is *the* answer we've been looking for—the answer that God intended for us all along.

What is it?

After God said, "I will give you a new heart and put a new spirit within you; and I will remove the heart of stone from your flesh and give you a heart of flesh"—after that, he promised this:

"I will put My Spirit within you."
– Ezekiel 36:27

Seven simple words, but they mean everything.

What does "I will put My Spirit within you" mean? It means God himself comes to live in us! Because the Holy Spirit is God. God the Father, God the Son, God the Holy Spirit—all three come to live in us. We become the place where God lives, forever.

STAGE 5: GOD LIVES IN US

This was God's plan for humanity all along. It's what we were designed for. God himself would come live in us, join us to himself, and become one with us— the closest, most intimate relationship possible. Why? So he could express his own life through us!

Paul said that this—"Christ in you"—was the very center of the message God called him to preach. Before he went to the cross, Jesus prayed for this very thing: that the Father would make us one with himself, and one with Jesus. One with God! It doesn't get any closer than that. Years later, Paul explained, "He who joins himself to the Lord becomes one spirit with him."

Wow. The next time you hear someone say, "You need to get closer to God," you can think to yourself, "I'm already one spirit with him. How much closer can I get?"

Let's pause for a minute and go back to the Saturn V. Its various stages were all essential to accomplish the main objective, to get astronauts to the moon. No one would get to the moon if any of the stages were missing.

God's new arrangement works exactly the same way. Do you see now why God had to accomplish stages 1-4 of his new arrangement? His objective was to live in us, and become one with us. To accomplish that, we had to be forgiven (Stage 1). If we weren't, we would have to pay for our sins ourselves, and be separated from him forever. We had to be cleansed (Stage 2). God is perfectly pure. He wasn't going to come to live permanently in an impure vessel. We had to have a new heart (Stage 3). God absolutely wasn't going to become one spirit with our old heart. We had to have his desires (Stage 4). God could only express his life through people who wanted the same things he wanted.

One more critical parallel: for the Saturn V, none of these stages were reversible. The rocket couldn't lift off, come back to earth, take off again, get into orbit, drop out of it, return to orbit, start toward the moon, come back for a bit—none of that was an option. Each stage had to be completely finished as planned, with no looking back.

Do you see as well why each stage of God's new arrangement had to be complete, permanent, and unchanging? If he was going to join our spirit to his and become permanently one with us, we couldn't be forgiven one minute and unforgiven the next. We had to be permanently forgiven. We couldn't be clean one minute and unclean the next. We had to be permanently clean for him to come live in us. We couldn't have a new heart one minute, an old heart the next, or both at the same time. We could only have one new creation heart for God to join himself to. Our deep inner being couldn't want what he wants one minute, and want what he doesn't the next. Our inner being had to be on the same page as his, permanently.

All of these things God had to accomplish completely

and irrevocably. There could be no looking back. That was the only way he could become one with us, live in us, and express himself fully through us.

The most important thing—by far—that God freely gives us is this: he himself comes to live in us. Because if the God of the universe comes to live in us, *that changes everything.*

If you stop and think about it, that makes complete sense. If the God of the universe comes to live in you, hasn't life's equation been totally altered? After all, who has the power to pull off the God kind of life—you, or God? The question answers itself.

The Apostle Paul indicated that for someone born of God, God living in them is *the* overriding reality:

> "I have been crucified with Christ [that is, the old Paul is dead; his heart of stone is gone] and it is no longer I who live, but Christ lives in me ..." – FIRST PART OF GALATIANS 2:20

Paul isn't saying he as a person has ceased to exist; he's certainly alive, with a new heart. But the one who is really living this life, he says, is Jesus living in him. Paul continues the thought:

> "... and the life which I now live in the flesh [that is, in this human body] I live by faith [by trusting] in the Son of God, who loved me and gave Himself up for me."
> – SECOND PART OF GALATIANS 2:20

Paul is saying, "Hey, I'm genuinely alive, and I live in this body, but the one who is really living here is Jesus. I live by trusting him living in me."

It shouldn't surprise us that this is what God was aiming at all along. Why? Because this is exactly the way Jesus lived on earth. We see Jesus in the gospels teaching and healing and doing miracles and we think, "Well, of course, he's God." But that's not how Jesus described what was going on. He said to his disciples, "The Father is living in me. The things you see me doing, it's actually the Father living his life through me."

In the Gospel of John, Jesus gives his famous illustration of the vine and the branches. He is the vine (the source of the life); we are the branches (through whom the life is visible). The branches can't produce anything on their own, because the vine is the life, not the branches.

When Jesus was on earth, though, the Father was the vine, and Jesus was the branch. The Father lived his life in and through Jesus. Jesus lived by faith in the Father living in him. The Father produced his works through him.

The Apostle John writes, "As [Jesus] is, so also are we in this world." We operate exactly the way Jesus did with the Father.

I knew all of this intellectually a long time before the Holy Spirit impressed the reality of it upon my heart. When that happened, life changed. I don't mean I never had troubling thoughts, or difficult feelings, or bad days. But the whole way I saw life changed. It wasn't about me performing, or making myself good enough anymore.

Basically, I started to live in this reality: when I walk into a room, God just walked into that room. (I'm not saying I'm God; I'm saying what he says, that he is the one living in me.)

If God just walked into the room, that totally takes the spotlight off of me. I don't have to worry anymore about *how am I coming across? What can I get out of this situation? How can these people benefit me? How unworthy do I feel? How am I performing?*

All of that becomes irrelevant! *God* just walked in the room. I'm simply the vessel he is living through. The life is from him. Remember how Jesus said, "I am the life"? This is that reality! When God walks into a room, the question is no longer *what would Jesus do?* That puts the burden on us to try hard to be like Jesus. Rather, the question is *what will Jesus do?* After all, he's living in us. Who is he going to bless? How is he going to love someone right here? How is he going to say something that lifts someone up?

It's totally natural. It's totally organic. We aren't trying hard to pull it off. It just flows. Christ loves through us. Christ serves through us. Christ forgives through us. It's not hard. It's natural. This is what our new heart wants to do, and what the One who lives in us is totally able to do. By faith, we step out, trusting him to do it.

I'm telling you, *this* is real living. I have plenty of growing yet to go in this, but I've experienced enough to know that life is way, way better when God himself is living it through us. It takes us completely out of the realm of self-focus, self-doubt, self-condemnation, and selfish living. Those things are swept aside. Life becomes an adventure. God just walked into the room!

This is how God designed us to operate all along. It is *the* answer to life.

"HOW CAN I LIVE THE RIGHT WAY?"

At this point, the astronauts are simply enjoying being on the moon. They're bounding around in 1/6 the gravity of Earth. They're planting flags. They're hitting golf balls. (Yes, the astronauts really did that. You can hit a golf ball a long way in low gravity!) They're collecting moon rocks. They're hopping in the moon buggy (OK, lunar rover) and going exploring.

In the same way, at this point we're just enjoying being in this new arrangement with God. He's done everything. We're just receiving it and enjoying it. And there are two specific things he wants us to enjoy—two more promises he fulfills.

ENJOYING GOD'S NEW ARRANGEMENT

Grasping the first one requires a paradigm shift. Because we can easily think this: God has forgiven us, cleansed us, given us a heart transplant, written his desires on our hearts, and come to live inside us; now the rest of it—actually living this thing out—is all up to us, right?

Wrong! The incredible thing about God's new arrangement is that it never switches over to being "all up to us." The new arrangement is a free gift, from start to finish.

The next free gift that God promised addresses this question: *how can I live the right way?* Usually following right on the heels of that question is this thought: *because I can't seem to do it very well.*

Right. I can't, either. None of us can. God knows that. What we don't realize is this: we weren't meant to be able to.

Think about it. Our lives are supposed to look like Jesus. Just as someone could look at Jesus walking on earth and conclude, "That's what God the Father is like," someone is supposed to look at our lives and conclude, "That's what Jesus is like."

But who can pull that off? Who can be loving enough to do that? Patient enough? Forgiving enough? Self-controlled enough? No one can.

Well, one person can. Jesus. And there's the answer to our question. It's no struggle for Jesus to live like Jesus. And he now lives inside us. That changes everything. That means that our entire life is operating in the realm of the supernatural.

The next promise God made under the new arrangement was this:

"I will put My Spirit within you *and cause you to walk in My statutes …*"   – Ezekiel 36:27

Whoa! Did you see that? After saying "I will put My Spirit within you"—God himself comes to live inside us—he then says, "and I will cause you to walk in my statutes."

Who is doing the causing here? God is! He doesn't say, "I will put My Spirit within you, and you will try hard to live like Jesus." No, he says, "*I* will cause you …"

45

This is a radically different view of the Christian life than we normally hear. The version we usually hear is something like, "OK, you're forgiven. So now live the right way. Try as hard as you can to live like Jesus would. See you on the other side one day."

Who is the "cause agent" in that scenario? You are! You have to cause yourself to live like Jesus. But that is *not* what God says his new arrangement with us would be. He says, "*I'm* going to cause you to do this." He is the cause agent, not us.

What does he say he will cause us to do? Walk in his statutes—his laws. Of course, we're not under the Law of Moses. (Paul actually says we died to it.) But the Jews in Ezekiel's time were, so God is speaking to them in language they would relate to. Put into our context, he would say, "I'm going to cause you to walk in my ways." Which means what? Trusting him and loving one another.

The rest of this promise was:

> "… and you will be careful to observe My ordinances." – Ezekiel 36:27

It's not a command; it's a promise. God is saying, "I'm going to cause you to walk in my ways, and when I do, you actually will walk in them. You actually will be trusting me, and loving others."

So how does he cause this? By coming to live inside us! Living his life inside us is completely natural for him. And so he "causes" us to walk in his ways.

Does this mean we're like robots now? No, not at all. This life he's designed is much more dynamic than that. But our role is not to produce the life by trying hard. Only he can produce the life. Our role is to walk by faith.

God has solved the problem of "How can I live the right way?" Like everything else in this new arrangement, it's a gift. We don't receive it by trying harder. We receive it by believing what he says. We live it by trusting in Christ in us.

Jesus said to his followers, "If you're worn out, come to me. I'll give you rest. My yoke is easy. My burden is light." If God seems burdensome, we aren't seeing him accurately! If the Christian life seems burdensome, we're trying to live it in a way God never intended!

How could Jesus say his yoke was easy, and his burden light? Because Jesus knew that he himself was going to come live in us. *That* makes it easy. Trying to keep all of God's commandments through our own effort, that's hard. Trying to be like Jesus, that's hard. Trying to do everything like Jesus would, that's hard. Trusting Jesus to live his own life through us—that's easy!

It goes back to Jesus's illustration of the vine and branches. The vine provides the life. That life flows through the branch and becomes fruit. But the branch isn't trying hard to produce fruit. It's simply letting the life (Jesus) flow through it.

Is this in some ways a mystery? Absolutely. But it's exactly how God designed us. It's how Jesus lived with the Father. And it's what God intended for us all along. The "abundant life" Jesus promised? This is it—God himself "causing" us. God himself living through us.

"I WISH I FELT CLOSE TO GOD" AND "I WISH I FELT REALLY LOVED"

If you asked a bunch of teens, "What do you want most in life?" a common answer might be "to feel really loved by someone I'm close to." We can get by without a lot of money, or a big house, or even a job to our liking, but to go through life without being close to someone, and loved—that's really hard.

It's not surprising that it's hard. We were made to be close and loved, and if we aren't experiencing that, something vital is missing. We feel it.

Starting in our teens, most of us begin looking for that one person who will give us that love. But sooner or later, we end up realizing that no one person can actually do that. Being in a good relationship is great, but our need to be loved is too deep for the finite, imperfect love of people to ultimately fulfill.

God knew this. He knew that we could only be fulfilled by his love. But we couldn't be fulfilled by a love that was far off—God loving us from a distance. No, we had to be close to him. Really close.

So under his new arrangement, God promised this:

"They will not teach again, each man his
neighbor and each man his brother, saying,
'Know the Lord,' for they will all know Me,
from the least of them to the greatest of them."
    – JEREMIAH 31:34

The Hebrew word "know" means having an intimate knowledge of, an experiential knowledge of. It's the word used in the Bible for sexual intercourse, as in "Jacob *knew* his wife Rachel, and she bore him a son." That's intimate knowledge. That's closeness.

God's answer to our need to be close to him is to make us close to him—as close as we can possibly be. It's not something we produce ourselves. It's totally a gift.

Right before he started his journey to the cross, Jesus asked the Father for two final things. The first was this: he asked that God the Father would make us one with himself and Jesus, just as the Father and Jesus were already one. In other words, he asked that we would have ultimate closeness with God.

God answers that prayer when we put our faith in Christ. He births a new spirit within us, and then he comes to live in us. And when that happens, as the Apostle Paul wrote, we "become one spirit with him."

We can't get any closer to God than that. We may or may not *feel* close at any given moment, but feelings only tell us how we're perceiving something, not the truth about it. The truth is, we *are* close to God, regardless of whether we *feel* it or not.

Why is that so vital? Because it means we aren't striving to create something—closeness to God—that's missing. Never again do we have to try to become close to God. We're already close to him. As close as we can get. Not surprisingly, counting on that reality is the key to *experiencing* our closeness with God more deeply.

This is how everything works under the new arrangement. God does it, and we learn to walk in what's already true. The critical thing is not that we feel close to God at any given moment, it's that we *are* close to God at every moment.

If you think about it, that makes total sense. You're in a relationship with a girl. But you're never quite sure where you stand. You always have to put your best foot forward, always have to be on guard to say and do the right thing. You want to be close, but the truth is you're having to try too hard. You're still wearing a mask. You're forcing it. It's not flowing naturally. Honestly, who wants to be in that kind of relationship? Who could ever get truly close in that relationship?

Unfortunately, this is exactly how so many people relate to God.

But under his new arrangement, God has bypassed all of that. We don't ever have to worry about any of that with God. We're already as close as we can be, and that will never, ever change. We can relax, and simply grow in getting to know God.

And what will we discover as we get to know him? We will discover that we are, at all times, being perfectly loved by the one who is closest to us.

God *is* love. His nature is to love. Always. Perfectly. If the Creator God is our God, it means that we are always being loved perfectly. The Bible says God loved us before we were born—from eternity past. In love he knit us in our mother's womb. In love he gave birth to us—the new birth his Spirit gives to our new spirit. More than anything, God shows us his love by sacrificing himself for us. God the Father sent God the Son to die for our sins, personally.

But God's love for us is not an external thing, with God loving us from afar. Just the opposite. Remember how Jesus asked the Father for two things before he went to the cross? The second thing Jesus asked was this: that the Father would put his love—the exact same love he has for Jesus—inside us. This incredible, infinite love that the Father and the Son have shared for all eternity, it's inside you. And inside me. God himself has come to live in us, and with his presence comes his perfect love.

What does this mean for us personally? In the same way that we can always count on our closeness to God, we can always count on being perfectly loved by God. His love is in us, and he's not going anywhere! Our emotions may not confirm that at any given moment, and our circumstances may not look like that, but that *is* the reality. It's the rock that we can always stand on.

But I still don't feel close to God or very loved by God, you might say. OK, fair enough, I can totally relate to that. I've spent much of my life not feeling very close to God, or loved by God, even though I wanted to.

This is where, once again, Christ in us is key. Because when Jesus prayed that the Father would make us one with himself, and put his love inside us, he tied those two things together. And I have found that, for me, they go hand in hand. As I know, in my actual experience, the reality of Christ in me, the love of God becomes my experienced reality as well. With the total assurance that God himself is the one living in me comes the assurance as well that I am, right now, being perfectly loved. We settle into the reality that Christ is the one living in and through us. And as we do, we settle into God's love. His love becomes our home, the place we hang out. And that's an incredible thing.

It's my hope that you will come to know the depths of God's love for you, too—a lot sooner than I did.

"WHAT'S THE REAL PURPOSE OF MY LIFE?"

None of us goes through life without asking (probably many times), "What's the purpose of my life?" The world has an answer to that question. It involves school, career, a nice house, finding a mate, etc. Its focus is on possessions, pleasure, maybe even power—none of which can ultimately satisfy.

God has a different answer. His plan, designed before you were born, doesn't have to do with external things. It has to do with life on the inside—his life in you. The God of the universe has come to live in you, to express himself, *through you*, to all creation.

That gives your life incredible meaning, far more than any meaning the world offers. It also gives you tremendous freedom. It means that you don't have to wait to discover or achieve God's purpose for your life. It's happening right now. He's living in you, and through you, right now. Which, when you think about it, also means this: you'll be living out God's purpose for you no matter what big decisions you make. If you're an accountant, Christ will be living through you. If you're an electrician, Christ will be living through you. If you're in Seattle, married with kids, or single in Houston, Christ will be living through you.

That takes a lot of pressure off! The real purpose of your life is the same, no matter what these externals may be. We can pursue what we want to in life, because Christ will daily be living out God's purpose through us in the midst of it.

So what is our role in God's grand purpose? It is huge, and it is this: we are partners with God. His part is producing the life—his life. Our part is being the channel for the life. We do that by simply believing God. The Holy Spirit reveals to us the things God has freely given us. The primary truth is Christ in us. We live, counting on the reality of this truth. We count on him. And as we do, Christ lives through us. We are *both* living this life.

The bottom line is that there's no formula, or series of steps, to deeply experience the reality of Christ in you. God doesn't work that way. Ultimately, it's his work. He will accomplish it. Look at Ezekiel 36:25-27 again:

> "I will sprinkle clean water on you, and you will be clean; I will cleanse you from all your filthiness and from all your idols. Moreover, I will give you a new heart and put a new spirit within you; and I will remove the heart of stone from your flesh and give you a heart of flesh. And I will put My Spirit within you and cause you to walk in My statutes ..."

What phrase leaps out from that passage? "*I will*"! Over and over, God says "I will do it."

I've found that when God makes "Christ in me" a deeper reality for me, I know perfectly well that God, and God alone, has done a work in me. It's never due to me doing "Christian" things—other than believing the truth God has already revealed. It's always the Holy Spirit revealing to me more of what I've already been freely given. He reveals this not just on an intellectual level, but a heart-knowing. And when he does, I start to live in this reality as never before. I wouldn't want to do anything else. It's too good!

Everyone who believes in Christ has been given everything in Christ already. All of God's free gifts are already ours. We may simply not know it yet. God is teaching us to walk in the truth of all that he's given us, and all that he is in us.

That's the key to walking by faith in Christ in us. The Holy Spirit shows us what is already true, and in our hearts we embrace it. We say, "Yes, that's the reality. I'll relax into that." When we're settled into God's reality, Christ flows freely through us.

So the work is God's. We're not being asked to pull this off ourselves. That's a huge relief! But we aren't robots. God has chosen to express himself through living people. He has chosen to partner with us. We cooperate with him by opening ourselves to receiving what the Holy Spirit has for us. We embrace the truth he shows us, we make ourselves available for him to live through, and we trust him living in us. It's not difficult. It's natural. It's exactly how God designed the new us to live.

When you step back and look at God's entire new arrangement with us, it's amazing. God has completely removed anything that would get in the way of our oneness with him, and of God himself living through us.

He's given us perfect forgiveness, perfect cleansing, a perfect new heart, perfect new desires, perfect oneness with him—and thus perfect fellowship with him, which simply means sharing his life. He's come inside us, to live his perfect life in us. None of that ever goes away. None of that ever changes. We don't have to worry about any of those things anymore! God has completely freed us to focus on his Son, who lives in us, and loves us perfectly.

So do I have any suggestions about living this supernatural life with Jesus? I do. Well, I have a couple of *don'ts*, actually. And one *do*. These aren't rules. They're simply things that you may find helpful in this adventure of God living in you, and through you.

DON'T DO THIS: *Don't ever measure yourself by how much religious stuff you're doing.* God says that you are "holy and blameless and faultless." Are you going to become more blameless and faultless by reading your Bible more? Praying more? Going to church more? God says he has "perfected [you] for all time" (Hebrews 10:14). How are you going to improve upon that by doing religious stuff?

I spent years judging myself by all my religious stuff. What a waste! Not that the activities themselves weren't profitable. Being around other believers was a good thing. Reading the Bible was a good thing. Memorizing scripture was a good thing (and something I highly recommend). The activities were profitable. What wasn't profitable was judging myself by all of that. I know a lot of scripture, but memorizing scripture didn't make God love me more. It didn't make me more acceptable to God. It didn't make God happier with me. And it never should have made me happier with myself.

I was perfectly fine all along. I just didn't know it. I was completely forgiven. I was completely clean. I had a new heart. Christ lived in me. I was perfectly loved at all times. I couldn't get more OK with God!

If God lays on your heart to memorize scripture, memorize it. If he gives you a desire to pray more, pray more. But don't judge yourself by these things. They don't make you more OK. What Christ did is what makes you OK, and you can't ever add to that.

DON'T DO THIS: *Don't focus on sin management.* The Christian life is *not* about sin management. "How can I change myself so that I stop sinning? What are the steps I can take? How can I be more committed?"

All of that is a dead end. Why? Because it puts the burden of getting our act together on us, which is *not* where it belongs. God said, "*I* will cause you to walk in My statutes," remember? But if our goal is to stop sinning, we're trying to cause ourselves to walk in his ways. It doesn't work. Paul discovered that for himself in Romans 7. He laid into the Galatians for this exact same thing. He said, "You began by the Spirit. Now you're trying to perfect yourself by the flesh [your own self-effort]? Are you guys nuts?"

Get your eyes off your own performance, and instead focus on Christ, and him in you. I love how our friend Ralph puts it: "The Christian's goal is not to stop sinning, but to start walking by faith in the Spirit of God inside."

Ask God to teach you to walk by faith in the Spirit of Christ, who lives in you. You can't produce the life of Jesus, but he can. That's what he does. He will live that life through you as you learn to walk by faith. And as he lives through you more fully, guess what? You will stop sinning.

And now, the one *do*.

DO THIS: Walk by faith. That's it. Live by faith. Over and over in the New Testament, we are told that "Those who are right with God walk by faith." Jesus told his disciples that this was the work God gave them to do: trust in him. Paul wrote to believers in Christ that in the exact same way they came to Christ (by faith), now they were to live in him.

We walk by faith!

So what does that mean exactly? It means that we live depending on and trusting in Christ who lives in us, and who lives his life through us. We believe what he says is true: he is living in us, and through us, right now. We aren't waiting to get "spiritual enough" to make it happen one day. We trust that it is happening *now*.

We are focusing, right now, on Christ and what he has already done, instead of focusing on ourselves and how we are doing with God. Through Christ, God has completely cleared the deck of anything we have to do to be OK with him. He has bypassed all that spiritual navel-gazing. He's set us free from that! There's nothing you can do to be more OK with God. You *are* OK with him—permanently. It has nothing to do with your performance. It's because of Jesus's performance. If you never do any "spiritual" things the rest of your life, you and God are fine. He's thrilled that you are his son.

We are focusing, right now, on Christ's ability, not ours. God himself lives in us. As I said before, that means our whole life operates in the realm of the supernatural. It's hard to love unconditionally, we think. Not for Jesus, it isn't, and he lives in us. Not only that, he has given us hearts that *want* to love others. We make ourselves available to him, and he does it through us. It's hard to forgive, we think. Not for Jesus, it isn't. We make ourselves available, and he forgives through us. *But I don't want to forgive,* you may think. Yes, you do! You have a new heart, birthed by the Spirit. Your feelings may not want to forgive, true. But your new heart, your inner man, loves to forgive. That's who he is.

Right now, we live by the Spirit, not by external rules. Our mindset isn't rules-based. It's relationship-based. We follow the Spirit. He leads us. He guides us. We ask him how he sees things, and he speaks to us in our new spirit. "Holy Spirit, here is this situation. Here is this emotion. Here is this temptation. What truth do you have to show me right now? What's the reality that you see?"

He does show us the truth, in this very moment. He reveals the things freely given to us. He reveals Christ in us. We embrace it, we make ourselves available to him, and Christ lives through us. The Spirit of Christ bears his fruit through us.

Walking by faith means walking in the truth, which means seeing things as God does. Our hearts have been made new, but our minds still need to be renewed. We still believe a lot of lies. "I'm no good! God will never do anything through me! He doesn't even like me!" The life of Jesus won't flow through lies.

Replacing lies with God's truth is vital. We embrace what God says is true. "I'm a righteous new creation. I'm the vessel God himself has chosen to live in. I'm his asset, not his liability. He loves me perfectly, and he is living through me right this minute, in these exact circumstances."

We are free, right now, to operate in complete liberty. That's why Jesus set us free! You're free to pursue the desires of your new heart. You're free to hear and follow the Spirit. You're free to let Jesus live through you in all his fullness. You're free to live the life God intended for you!

But if I have all this freedom, won't I live a life of sin? No! That's the beauty of God's new arrangement. He's given you a new heart. His Spirit has come to live in you. Deep down, you don't *want* to live a life of sin. It's completely incompatible with who you are, it can't satisfy you, and so you wouldn't stay there long-term, anyway. God has given us something far better—his life in us.

It doesn't get any more practical than this. It changes everything. Now you're living by faith. God has moved heaven and earth just so he could come live inside you. By faith, you're letting him live through you, and in the process, fulfilling everything you were created to be.

Before I wrap this letter up, I mentioned earlier that I would address an important question: "If I have a new heart, why do I still sin?" I've thought of a couple more questions that might be helpful to answer as well. Here goes.

SO ARE YOU SAYING THAT GOD DOESN'T JUST *SEE* ME AS RIGHTEOUS, THAT I ACTUALLY *AM* RIGHTEOUS?

Yes, that's exactly what I'm saying, because that's exactly what God says. Our hearts wouldn't have been ready to become one with God if he simply *declared* us righteous. He had to *make* us righteous. And that's what God says he did. Paul writes,

> He [God the Father] made him [Jesus] who knew no sin to be sin on our behalf, so that we might become the righteousness of God in Him. – 2 Corinthians 5:21

He says,

> For as through the one man's disobedience the many were made sinners, so also through the obedience of the One the many will be made righteous. – Romans 5:19

He says that our new man was

> created after the likeness of God in true righteousness and holiness. – Ephesians 4:24

The Apostle John wrote:

> The one who practices righteousness is righteous, just as [Jesus] is righteous.
> – 1 John 3:7

John doesn't say that God just sees us as righteous. He says we are righteous, *just as Jesus is righteous*. We can't get any more righteous than that!

God had to make us righteous to accomplish his purpose for our lives. We are righteous not as a result of our behavior, but as a result of our new birth. The Spirit gave birth to our new spirit. He could only give birth to someone with his own nature. That's us!

SO IF I'M NOW RIGHTEOUS IN MY INNER BEING, WHY DO I STILL SIN?

Ah, that's a pretty important question, isn't it? God provides a very specific answer, and he makes it very clear, if we read carefully. He says in Romans 7:14-25 that the reason we find ourselves being dragged down by this power called sin is that we live in bodies that haven't yet been changed. Our inner being has been changed, but "the members of our body" haven't been. That's where the power of sin is located now, in the members of our physical body (which includes our physical brain). Those members are programmed to sin (to seek life on their own, independent of God).

The solution is not us trying harder not to sin. That's what Paul was trying (and failing) to do in Romans 7. It doesn't work. God never intended for it to work. The solution is living by faith in Christ in us. Jesus never has a problem not sinning.

The very good news is that your heart is completely on God's side now. Your new heart wants what God wants. That's why Paul makes the astounding statement (twice!) that when he finds himself sinning, it's not him doing it, it's the power of sin that lives in the members of his unchanged body. Whoa! That's pretty radical. And that's one reason why there's no condemnation from God for it. God knows we don't want to be sinning, not in our deepest being. So we don't have to beat ourselves up over it, either. We thank God we're already forgiven and move on. Jesus has people to love through us.

GOD SAYS THAT HE AND I ARE NOW ONE SPIRIT. BUT WHEN I SIN, DON'T I TEMPORARILY LOSE THAT CONNECTION WITH GOD?

No. Absolutely not. You never stop being one with him. When you sin, God doesn't go anywhere, and neither do you. You're still one spirit with him, which is as close as you can get. You still share in God's divine nature. When you sin, you're simply not walking in the truth of who you now are, and who Christ is in you. God wants to teach you to walk in the truth.

Jesus put away the sin issue between you and God. You're completely forgiven. God doesn't even remember your sin. You don't have to do anything to be "restored" to God. Christ's sacrifice already restored you. You don't have to add anything to it. You *can't* add anything to it. Does that mean we are taking sin lightly? No, not at all.

It means we're taking everything Jesus accomplished in his death and resurrection *very* seriously.

What God has done for us in Christ bypasses any steps we might try to take to get back to God. Those steps were necessary under the Law of Moses, yes, but not anymore. We live in the freedom of being completely forgiven, completely restored, completely made a new person, and completely having God live in us. Like the completed steps of the Saturn V rocket, we don't have to go back and redo any of that. It's done. Instead, God is teaching us to simply walk in the reality of all he's already done for us, and in us.

So let's go back to the questions I posed at the very beginning of this letter. They're vital questions, and we all have at least some of them. Here are God's answers:

> - *"Sometimes I feel bad about things I've done."* If you've believed in Christ, God has forgiven you 100%. You can let the past go.
> - *"Sometimes I feel … stained."* God has cleansed you 100%. You're as clean as you can be.
> - *"I wish I liked myself more."* God has given you a heart transplant and you are a totally new person, perfectly righteous, like him. The God of the universe is thrilled that you are his child. You are exactly who he wants you to be.

➤ *"Do I really want to do what's right?"* God has written his desires on your heart; deep down, you want what he wants.

➤ *"I just wish I had THE answer to life."* God himself has come to live in you forever; that is the answer.

➤ *"How can I live the right way?"* God himself will cause you to walk in his ways.

➤ *"I wish I felt close to God."* You are, right now, as close to God as someone can be, as close as Jesus is to the Father.

➤ *"I wish I felt really loved."* You are, right now, perfectly, infinitely, passionately loved by God. God the Father loves you exactly the same way he loves Jesus.

And this last question, which wraps it all up: *"What's the real purpose of my life?"* Your life's purpose is to be one with God, to know him and his love, and to be the expression of God to all the world as he lives through you.

Does God have an answer to all the deep questions we have about life? Yeah, he really does. The answer is Christ in us. God himself comes to live his own life in us.

After he took five loaves of bread and used them to feed many thousands, Jesus told the people around him what the miracle really meant. He said, "I'm the bread of life; the one who comes to me will not be hungry, and the one who believes in me will never be thirsty." For the longest time I read that verse and thought, "That may be true, but I'm still hungering and thirsting."

I don't have to hunger anymore. I don't have to thirst anymore. I've found that the reality of Jesus living in me really can fill me. He offers that to both of us.

There's one major difference between us and the Apollo astronauts who landed on the moon. Successfully navigating all the stages of the Saturn V rocket enabled them to experience the moon for one day, or two, or three. God successfully accomplishing all the stages of his new arrangement enables us to experience oneness with God, and the fullness of his life, for eternity. Going to the moon was a pretty great adventure. But it's nothing compared to what we have. Ours is an adventure that has no equal: God himself living through us.

———

It's been such a thrill seeing you grow and mature over the years, especially the last couple. I'm so proud of the young man that you are becoming, and for how you've thrown yourself into numerous valuable endeavors. I'm so privileged to experience this time in your life with you and walk alongside you. I look forward to what God has in store for each of us!

I love you.
Dad

SOME HELPFUL STUFF

So, you've finished this letter. Maybe you'd like to verify that this is what the Bible actually says, or explore God's new arrangement more, or simply reinforce what you've read. After all, it's easy to fall back into our old way of thinking about ourselves and God. I've attached this section to help. Here's what you'll find:

> Bible verses I've referred to in this letter. Looking through these verses will help you more deeply see God's truth that I've been talking about.
> Some longer New Testament passages that answer the question, "Are there large sections of the New Testament that teach this, and not just individual verses?" The answer to that is a resounding *yes*!
> Two simple sheets to help internalize God's truth: "Who I Am Now" and "Who Christ Is In Me." To walk in the truth, we have to be grounded in the truth.

> ➤ A few additional resources that are helpful in learning more. I especially recommend the short videos, which are quite easy to digest.

BIBLE REFERENCES

Here are verses from the Bible that go along with the points I made in the letter. I'm putting these in order of the sections of the letter, starting with the first.

A LITTLE HISTORY ABOUT RULE-KEEPING

Humanity broke its connection with God: "Therefore, just as through one man sin entered into the world, and death through sin, and so death spread to all men, because all sinned ..." – Romans 5:12

God and Abraham: "Now the Lord said to Abram, 'Go forth from your country, and from your relatives and from your father's house, to the land which I will show you; and I will make you a great nation ... and in you all the families of the earth will be blessed.'"
 – Genesis 12:1-3

God and Abraham: "And He took him outside and said, 'Now look toward the heavens, and count the stars, if you are able to count them.' And He said to him, 'So shall your descendants be.' Then he believed in the Lord; and He reckoned it to him as righteousness."
 – Genesis 15:5-6

The old arrangement under the Law of Moses: "'Now it shall be, if you diligently obey the Lord your God, being careful to do all His commandments which I command you today, the Lord your God will set you high above all the nations of the earth. All these blessings will come upon you and overtake you if you obey the Lord your God ... But it shall come about, if you do not obey the Lord your God, to observe to do all His commandments and His statutes with which I charge you today, that all these curses will come upon you and overtake you ...'"
– DEUTERONOMY 28:1-2, 15

God's standard is perfection: "'Therefore you are to be perfect, as your heavenly Father is perfect.'"
– MATTHEW 5:48

God gave the Law to show people their sin: "... by the works of the Law none of mankind will be justified in His sight; for through the Law comes knowledge of sin." – ROMANS 3:20

God provided a new way to be connected to him, not based on human effort: "But now apart from the Law the righteousness of God has been revealed, being witnessed by the Law and the Prophets, but it is the righteousness of God through faith in Jesus Christ for all who believe ..."
– ROMANS 3:21-22A

The Law of Moses was a temporary arrangement: "When He said, 'A new covenant,' He has made the first obsolete. But whatever is becoming obsolete and growing old is ready to disappear." – HEBREWS 8:13

Also, "He takes away the first in order to establish the second." – HEBREWS 10:9B

A NEW ARRANGEMENT

We are no longer under the Law of Moses: "Therefore, my brethren, you also were made to die to the Law through the body of Christ, so that you might be joined to another, to Him who was raised from the dead, in order that we might bear fruit for God.... But now we have been released from the Law, having died to that by which we were bound, so that we serve in newness of the Spirit and not in oldness of the letter." – ROMANS 7:4, 6

"SOMETIMES I FEEL BAD ABOUT THINGS I'VE DONE"

The penalty for sin is death: "For the wages of sin is death, but the free gift of God is eternal life in Christ Jesus our Lord." – ROMANS 6:23, ESV

God chose to pay the penalty for sin himself and offer forgiveness as a free gift: "For everyone has sinned; we all fall short of God's glorious standard. Yet God, in his grace, freely makes us right in his sight. He did this through Christ Jesus when he freed us from the penalty for our sins. For God presented Jesus as the sacrifice for sin. People are made right with God when they believe that Jesus sacrificed his life, shedding his blood."   – ROMANS 3:23-25A, NLT

All we can do is receive the gift: "'For God so loved the world, that He gave His only Son, so that everyone who believes in Him will not perish, but have eternal life.'"   – JOHN 3:16

All of our sins are forgiven: "When you were dead in your transgressions and the uncircumcision of your flesh, He made you alive together with Him, having forgiven us all our transgressions ..."   – COLOSSIANS 2:13

Christ has put away the sin issue between us and God: "... but now once at the consummation of the ages [Christ] has been manifested to put away sin by the sacrifice of Himself."   – HEBREWS 9:26B

God doesn't treat us according to our sins: "'Blessed are those whose lawless deeds have been forgiven, and whose sins have been covered. Blessed is the man whose sin the Lord will not take into account.'"
   – ROMANS 4:7-8

There's never any condemnation for our sins: "Therefore there is now no condemnation for those who are in Christ Jesus."   – ROMANS 8:1

Paul forgot what lay behind and moved ahead:
"Brethren, I do not regard myself as having laid hold
of it yet; but one thing I do: forgetting what lies
behind and reaching forward to what lies ahead ..."
– Philippians 3:13

"SOMETIMES I FEEL ... STAINED"

We are thoroughly cleansed by God: "Such were some
of you; but you were washed, but you were sanctified,
but you were justified in the name of the Lord Jesus
Christ and in the Spirit of our God."   – 1 Corinthians 6:11

Also, "He saved us, not on the basis of deeds which
we have done in righteousness, but according to His
mercy, by the washing of regeneration and renewing
by the Holy Spirit ..."   – Titus 3:5

We are clean and have perfect access to God:
"Therefore, brethren, since we have confidence to
enter the holy place by the blood of Jesus ... let us
draw near with a sincere heart in full assurance of
faith, having our hearts sprinkled clean from an evil
conscience and our bodies washed with pure water."
– Hebrews 10:19, 22

"I WISH I LIKED MYSELF MORE"

How we are born into the world: "And you were dead
in your trespasses and sins, in which you formerly

walked according to the course of this world, according to the prince of the power of the air, of the spirit that is now working in the sons of disobedience. Among them we too all formerly lived in the lusts of our flesh, indulging the desires of the flesh and of the mind, and were by nature children of wrath, even as the rest."   – EPHESIANS 2:1-3

Also: "... remember that you were at that time separate from Christ, excluded from the commonwealth of Israel, and strangers to the covenants of promise, having no hope and without God in the world."
   – EPHESIANS 2:12

God births a new spirit within us: "Jesus answered, 'Truly, truly, I say to you, unless one is born of water and the Spirit he cannot enter into the kingdom of God. That which is born of the flesh is flesh, and that which is born of the Spirit is spirit.'"   – JOHN 3:5-6

We are actually born of God: "But as many as received Him, to them He gave the right to become children of God, even to those who believe in His name, who were born, not of blood nor of the will of the flesh nor of the will of man, but of God."
   – JOHN 1:12-13

Also, "Whoever believes that Jesus is the Christ is born of God, and whoever loves the Father loves the child born of Him."   – 1 JOHN 5:1

Our old man is gone: "… knowing this, that our old self [literally, *man*] was crucified with Him, in order that our body of sin might be done away with, so that we would no longer be slaves to sin …"   – Romans 6:6

Our new man is holy and righteous: "… the new self, created after the likeness of God in true righteousness and holiness."   – Ephesians 4:24, esv

We are sharers in God's own nature: "For by these He has granted to us His precious and magnificent promises, so that by them you may become partakers of the divine nature, having escaped the corruption that is in the world by lust."   – 2 Peter 1:4

God has perfected us for all time: "For by one offering He has perfected for all time those who are sanctified."   – Hebrews 10:14

We are completely accepted by God: "Therefore, accept one another, just as Christ also accepted us to the glory of God."
   – Romans 15:7

"DO I REALLY WANT TO DO WHAT'S RIGHT?"

Our new heart is on the same page as God:
"For I joyfully concur with the law of God in the inner man …"   – Romans 7:22

Jesus left us with two commandments:
"'This is My commandment, that you love one another, just as I have loved you.'"   – John 15:12

Also, "This is His commandment, that we believe in the name of His Son Jesus Christ, and love one another, just as He commanded us."   – 1 John 3:23

Also, "If, however, you are fulfilling the royal law according to the Scripture, 'You shall love your neighbor as yourself,' you are doing well."   – James 2:8

Also, "Owe nothing to anyone except to love one another; for he who loves his neighbor has fulfilled the law." – Romans 13:8

"I JUST WISH I HAD *THE* ANSWER TO LIFE"

Christ in us is the key: "... the mystery which has been hidden from the past ages and generations, but has now been manifested to His saints, to whom God willed to make known what is the riches of the glory of this mystery among the Gentiles, which is Christ in you ..."   – Colossians 1:26-27

The Holy Spirit comes to live in us: "'I will ask the Father, and He will give you another Helper, that He may be with you forever; that is the Spirit of truth, whom the world cannot receive, because it does not see Him or know Him, but you know Him because He abides with you and will be in you.'"   – John 14:16-17

77

Christ comes to live in us: "'In that day you will know that I am in My Father, and you in Me, and I in you.'"
   – John 14:20

The Father comes to live in us: "Jesus answered and said to him, 'If anyone loves Me, he will keep My word; and My Father will love him, and We will come to him and make Our abode with him.'"   – John 14:23

God makes himself one with us: "'I do not ask on behalf of these alone, but for those also who believe in Me through their word; that they may all be one; even as You, Father, are in Me and I in You, that they also may be in Us ...'"   – John 17:20-21

We are one spirit with God. "But the one who joins himself to the Lord is one spirit with Him."
   – 1 Corinthians 6:17

The Father lived through Jesus: "Jesus said to him, 'Have I been so long with you, and yet you have not come to know Me, Philip? He who has seen Me has seen the Father; how can you say, "Show us the Father"? Do you not believe that I am in the Father, and the Father is in Me? The words that I say to you I do not speak on My own initiative, but the Father abiding in Me does His works. Believe Me that I am in the Father and the Father is in Me; otherwise believe because of the works themselves.'"
   – John 14:9-11

We live the same way Jesus lived: "... as He is, so also are we in this world."   – 1 John 4:17

We receive life just as Jesus did: "As the living Father sent me, and I live because of the Father, so whoever feeds on me, he also will live because of me."
   – John 6:57, esv

Jesus is the vine, we are the branches: "'Abide in Me, and I in you. As the branch cannot bear fruit of itself unless it abides in the vine, so neither can you unless you abide in Me. I am the vine, you are the branches; he who abides in Me and I in him, he bears much fruit, for apart from Me you can do nothing.'"
   – John 15:4-5

Jesus is the life: "Jesus said to him, 'I am the way, and the truth, and the life; no one comes to the Father but through Me.'"   – John 14:6

"HOW CAN I LIVE THE RIGHT WAY?"

We live by simply trusting: "The righteous shall live by faith."   – Romans 1:17b, esv

Also, "The righteous shall live by faith."
   – Galatians 3:11b, esv

Also, "But My righteous one will live by faith."
   – Hebrews 10:38

Also, "Therefore, as you have received Christ Jesus the Lord, so walk in Him …" – Colossians 2:6

Jesus's yoke is easy: "'Come to Me, all who are weary and heavy-laden, and I will give you rest. Take My yoke upon you and learn from Me, for I am gentle and humble in heart, and you will find rest for your souls. For My yoke is easy and My burden is light.'"
– Matthew 11:28-30

"I WISH I FELT CLOSE TO GOD" AND "I WISH I FELT REALLY LOVED"

We are as close to God as we can be: "But the one who joins himself to the Lord is one spirit with Him."
– 1 Corinthians 6:17

God is love: "The one who does not love does not know God, for God is love." – 1 John 4:8

God loves us deeply and wants us to know his love: "… just as He chose us in Him before the foundation of the world, that we would be holy and blameless before Him. In love He predestined us to adoption as sons through Jesus Christ to Himself, according to the kind intention of His will, to the praise of the glory of His grace, which He freely bestowed on us in the Beloved." – Ephesians 1:4-6

Also, "But God demonstrates His own love toward us, in that while we were yet sinners, Christ died for us." – Romans 5:8

Christ living in us shows us the fullness of God's love: "'... I in them and You in Me, that they may be perfected in unity, so that the world may know that You sent Me, and loved them, even as You have loved Me.... and I have made Your name known to them, and will make it known, so that the love with which You loved Me may be in them, and I in them.'"
  – JOHN 17:23, 26

"WHAT'S THE REAL PURPOSE OF MY LIFE?"

We are the channel for God's life: "But we have this treasure in earthen vessels, so that the surpassing greatness of the power will be of God and not from ourselves ..." – 2 CORINTHIANS 4:7

The Holy Spirit reveals to us the things we've been freely given: "Now we have received, not the spirit of the world, but the Spirit who is from God, so that we may know the things freely given to us by God ..."
  – 1 CORINTHIANS 2:12

Our part is believing: "Therefore they said to Him, 'What shall we do, so that we may work the works of God?' Jesus answered and said to them, 'This is the work of God, that you believe in Him whom He has sent.'" – JOHN 6:28-29

Also, "'I have been crucified with Christ; and it is no longer I who live, but Christ lives in me; and the life which I now live in the flesh I live by faith in the Son of God, who loved me and gave Himself up for me.'" – Galatians 2:20

We've been given everything already: "Blessed be the God and Father of our Lord Jesus Christ, who has blessed us with every spiritual blessing in the heavenly places in Christ …" – Ephesians 1:3

Also, "… seeing that His divine power has granted to us everything pertaining to life and godliness, through the true knowledge of Him who called us by His own glory and excellence." – 2 Peter 1:3

We are holy, blameless, and beyond reproach: "… just as He chose us in Him before the foundation of the world, that we would be holy and blameless before Him." – Ephesians 1:4

Also: "… yet He has now reconciled you in His body of flesh through death, in order to present you before Him holy and blameless and beyond reproach …"
– Colossians 1:22

We have been perfected for all time: "For by one offering He has perfected for all time those who are sanctified." – Hebrews 10:14

The Christian's goal is not to stop sinning, but to start walking by faith in the Spirit of God inside: "But I say, walk by the Spirit, and you will not carry out the desire of the flesh." – Galatians 5:16

Also: "You foolish Galatians, who has bewitched you, before whose eyes Jesus Christ was publicly portrayed as crucified? This is the only thing I want to find out from you: did you receive the Spirit by the works of the Law, or by hearing with faith? Are you so foolish? Having begun by the Spirit, are you now being perfected by the flesh?"   – GALATIANS 3:1-3

God has freed us to be Christ-conscious: "… fixing our eyes on Jesus, the author and perfecter of faith …"
   – HEBREWS 12:2

We live in freedom: "It was for freedom that Christ set us free; therefore keep standing firm and do not be subject again to a yoke of slavery."   – GALATIANS 5:1

We are led by the Spirit. "For all who are being led by the Spirit of God, these are sons of God."   – ROMANS 8:14

God intends for us to hear his voice: "'My sheep hear My voice, and I know them, and they follow Me …'"
   – JOHN 10:27

We walk in God's truth: "I have no greater joy than this, to hear of my children walking in the truth."
   – 3 JOHN 1:4

Also: "So Jesus was saying to those Jews who had believed Him, 'If you continue in My word, then you are truly disciples of Mine; and you will know the truth, and the truth will make you free.'"   – JOHN 8:31-32

SO IF I'M NOW RIGHTEOUS IN MY INNER BEING, WHY DO I STILL SIN?

Our inner being has been changed, but the power of sin still exists in the members of our physical body: "For I do not understand what I am doing; for I am not practicing what I want to do, but I do the very thing I hate. However, if I do the very thing I do not want to do, I agree with the Law, that the Law is good. But now, no longer am I the one doing it, but sin that dwells in me." – ROMANS 7:15-17

Also: "For the good that I want, I do not do, but I practice the very evil that I do not want. But if I do the very thing I do not want, I am no longer the one doing it, but sin that dwells in me." – ROMANS 7:19-20

Also: "I find then the principle that evil is present in me, the one who wants to do good. For I joyfully agree with the law of God in the inner person, but I see a different law in the parts of my body waging war against the law of my mind, and making me a prisoner of the law of sin, the law which is in my body's parts." – ROMANS 7:21-23

WHEN I SIN, DON'T I TEMPORARILY LOSE MY CONNECTION WITH GOD?

Through the cross, Jesus has permanently connected us to God: "… but [Christ], having offered one sacrifice for sins for all time, sat down at the right hand of God … For by one offering He has perfected for all time those who are sanctified." – Hebrews 10:12, 14

Also, "Now where there is forgiveness of these things, an offering for sin is no longer required."
– Hebrews 10:18

God makes himself one with us: "But the one who joins himself to the Lord is one spirit with Him."
– 1 Corinthians 6:17

END OF THE LETTER

Jesus is the bread of life: "Jesus said to them, 'I am the bread of life; he who comes to Me will not hunger, and he who believes in Me will never thirst.'"
– John 6:35

Bible Passages for Reading

Concerning the preceding section of verses, someone could say, "You can always pick individual verses out of context to prove a point." That's true! So, do large sections of the New Testament teach what God promises in his new arrangement with us? Yes, absolutely. The following passages are some of them. They are excellent reading to get God's big picture.

- *The Gospel of John*, chapters 14 through 17
- *Paul's Letter to the Romans*, chapters 3 through 8
- *Paul's Second Letter to the Corinthians*, chapters 3 through 5
- *Paul's Letter to the Galatians*, verse 2:16 through chapter 5
- *Paul's Letter to the Ephesians*, chapters 1 through 3
- *Paul's Letter to the Colossians*, verse 1:12 through verse 3:4
- *The Letter to the Hebrews,* verse 8:7 through verse 10:22

WHO I AM NOW

TRUTH	VERSE(S)
Born of God—His child	John 1:12-13; John 3:5-6
A new creation	2 Corinthians 5:17
The righteousness of God	Romans 5:19; 2 Corinthians 5:21; 1 John 3:7
One spirit with God	1 Corinthians 6:17
The place where God lives	1 Corinthians 3:16
The person Christ lives through	Galatians 2:20
Perfected for all time	Hebrews 10:14
Complete	Colossians 2:10
Created in righteousness and holiness	Ephesians 4:24
A sharer in the divine nature	2 Peter 1:4
Holy, blameless, and above reproach	Ephesians 1:4; Colossians 1:22
Beloved by God	Romans 1:7; 1 John 3:1
A saint—a holy one	Romans 1:7
Seated with Christ in the heavenlies	Ephesians 2:6
A citizen of heaven	Philippians 3:20
Chosen by God	Ephesians 1:4
Christ's friend	John 15:14
An heir of God with Christ	Romans 8:17; Galatians 4:7
God's workmanship	Ephesians 2:10

WHO CHRIST IS IN ME

TRUTH	VERSE(S)
God Himself	John 1:1
The Life	John 11:25; 14:6
The Way	John 14:6
The Truth	John 14:6
The Light	John 1:4; 8:12
Wisdom from God	1 Corinthians 1:30
Righteousness	1 Corinthians 1:30
Sanctification	1 Corinthians 1:30
Redemption	1 Corinthians 1:30
Love	1 Timothy 1:14
Lord	1 Corinthians 8:6
Savior	Titus 3:13
The Resurrection	John 11:25
The Power of God	1 Corinthians 1:24
The Bread of Life	John 6:35
The author and perfecter of faith	Hebrews 12:2
The treasure of God's glory	2 Corinthians 4:6
God's mystery	Colossians 2:2
All	Colossians 3:11

WHERE CAN YOU LEARN MORE?

There's tons of great material out there on God's new arrangement with us. I highly recommend any videos from the websites of Ralph Harris (ralphharris.org) and Andrew Farley (andrewfarley.org). Ralph, in particular, has a bunch of great two- to five-minute videos that are really easy to watch. He also has a bunch of great blog posts on Facebook.

A few years ago I wrote another book on God's new arrangement with us. It's more detailed but still short and very readable. Look into it sometime:

If Jesus Loves Me Why Isn't This Working?,
    David Gregory

Three other great books on this subject are:

The Rest of the Gospel: When the Partial Gospel Has Worn You Out, Dan Stone and David Gregory

The Perfect You: God's Invitation to Live from the Heart, Andrew Farley and Tim Chalas

God's Outstanding Opinion of You: Understanding Your Identity Will Change Your Life, Ralph Harris

There are a lot of good books about the validity of Christianity and the Bible. I especially like these, which are also very readable:

Mere Christianity, C.S. Lewis

More Than a Carpenter, Josh and Sean McDowell (very readable)

Several books by Lee Strobel: *The Case for Christ*, *The Case for Faith*, *The Case for a Creator*, and *In Defense of Jesus*

ABOUT DAVID GREGORY

David Gregory has been teaching and writing about God's new arrangement with us for years. His seven novels include *The New York Times'* extended best-seller *Dinner with a Perfect Stranger* and Christy Award finalist *The Last Christian.* Three of his novels have been made into feature films. David's nonfiction books include *The Rest of the Gospel: When the Partial Gospel Has Worn You Out* and *If Jesus Loves Me Why Isn't This Working?* A native of Texas, David holds master's degrees from Dallas Theological Seminary and The University of North Texas. He was formerly on the ministry team of Insight for Living, the Bible teaching ministry of Charles Swindoll.

For more information about David, to invite him to speak, or to simply connect with him, find him at:

www.davidgregorybooks.com

facebook.com/DavidGregoryAuthor

twitter.com/davidgregorys

OTHER BOOKS
BY DAVID GREGORY

Made in the USA
Columbia, SC
13 February 2024

31477024R00054